AF587448

Would you rather...

Christoph Elias Meier & Mara Züst
with drawings by Carolina Cerbaro

Would you rather

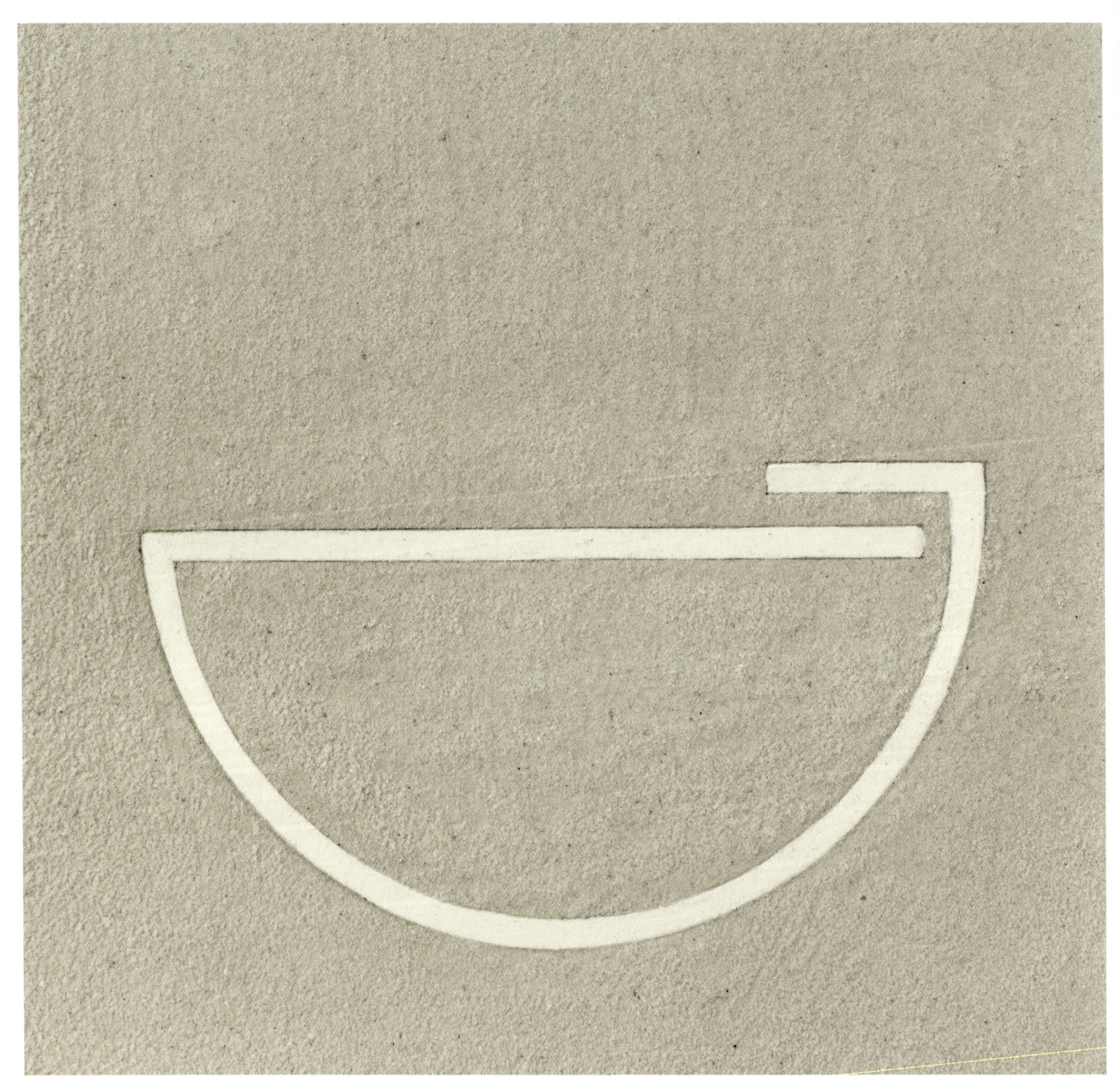

be a twisted corner of a mouth,

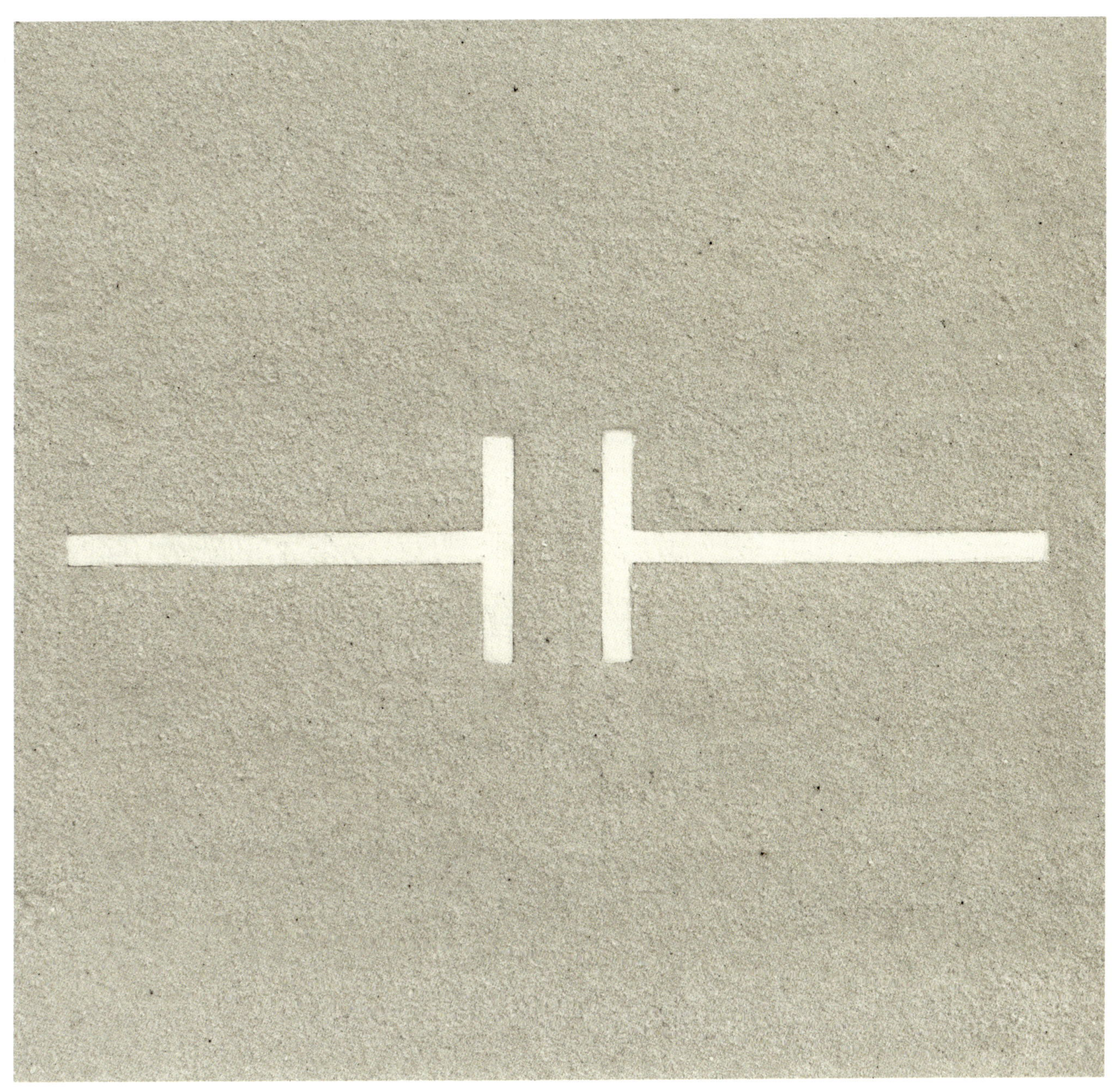

a furrow of a brow,

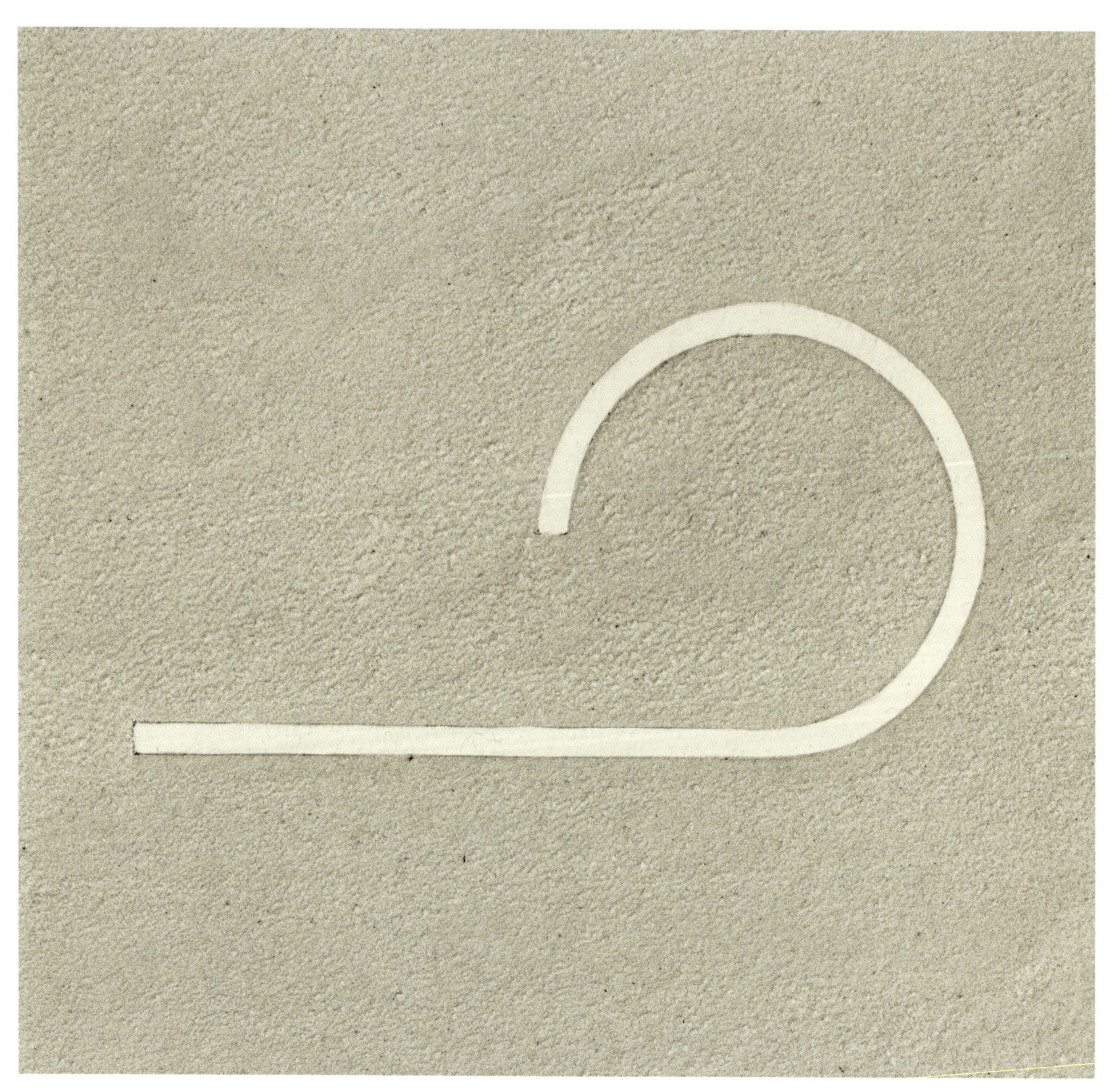

a curled-up tongue,

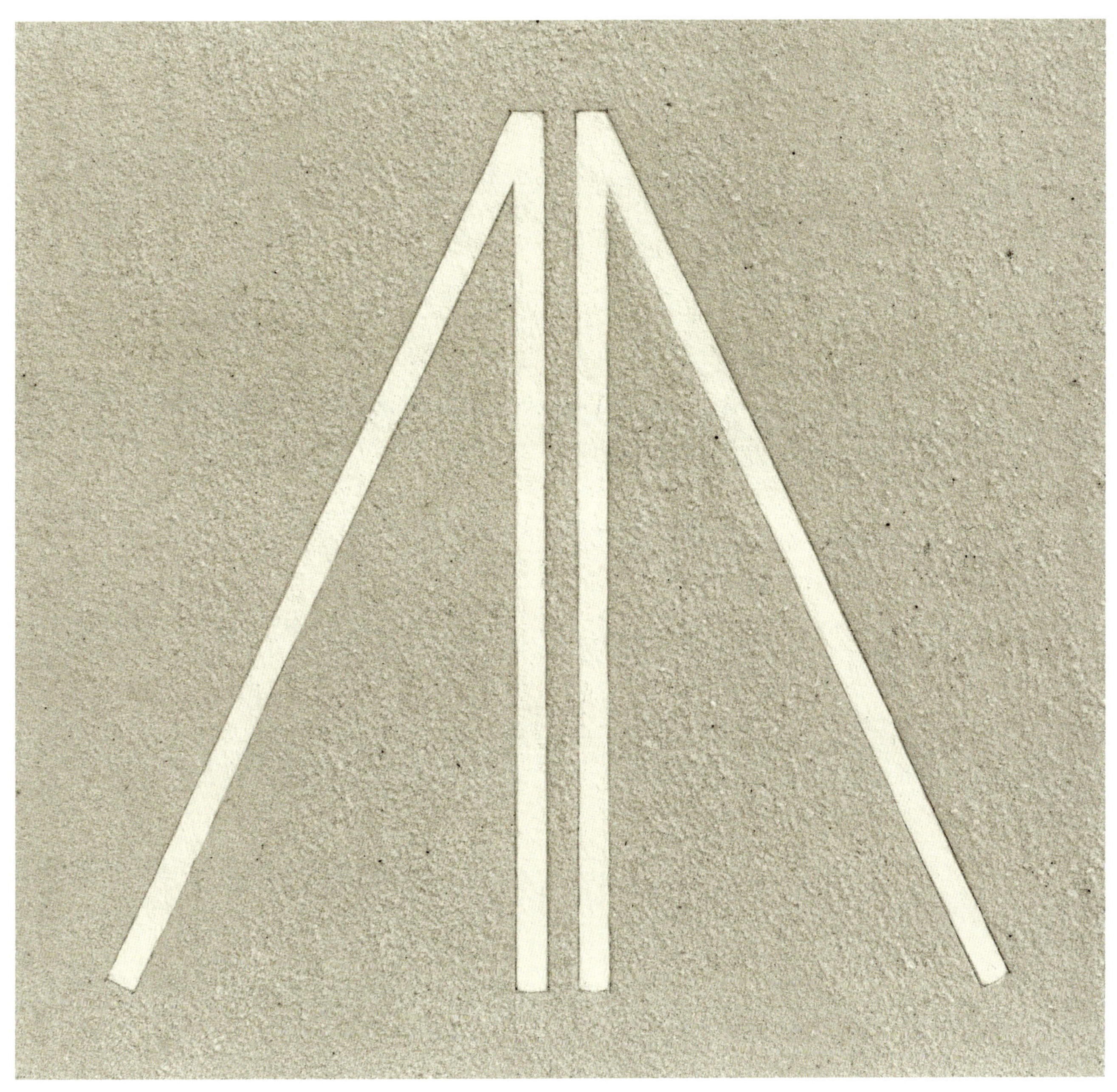

or a crocodile tear?

Would you rather

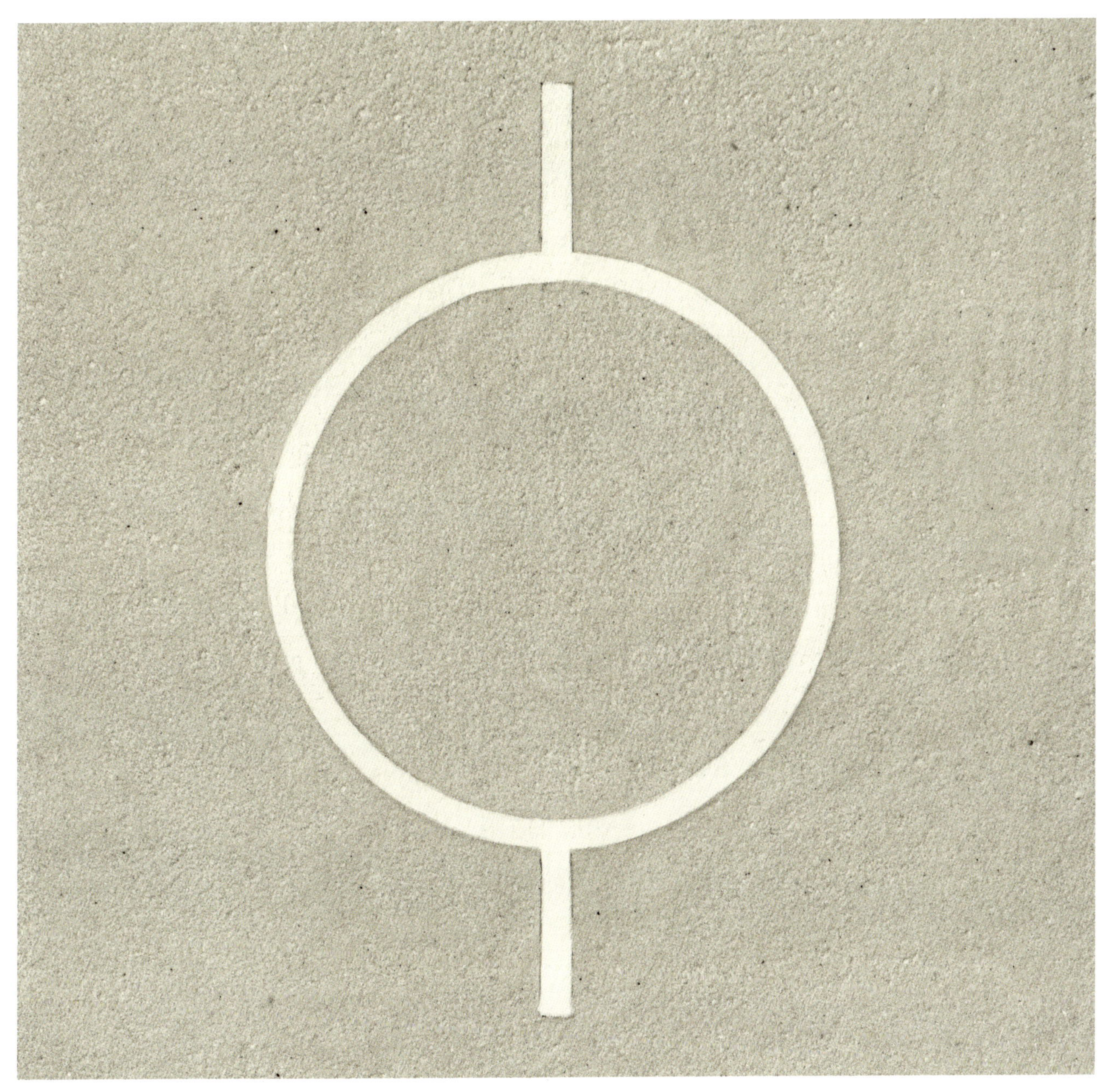

float as a satellite orbiting the earth,

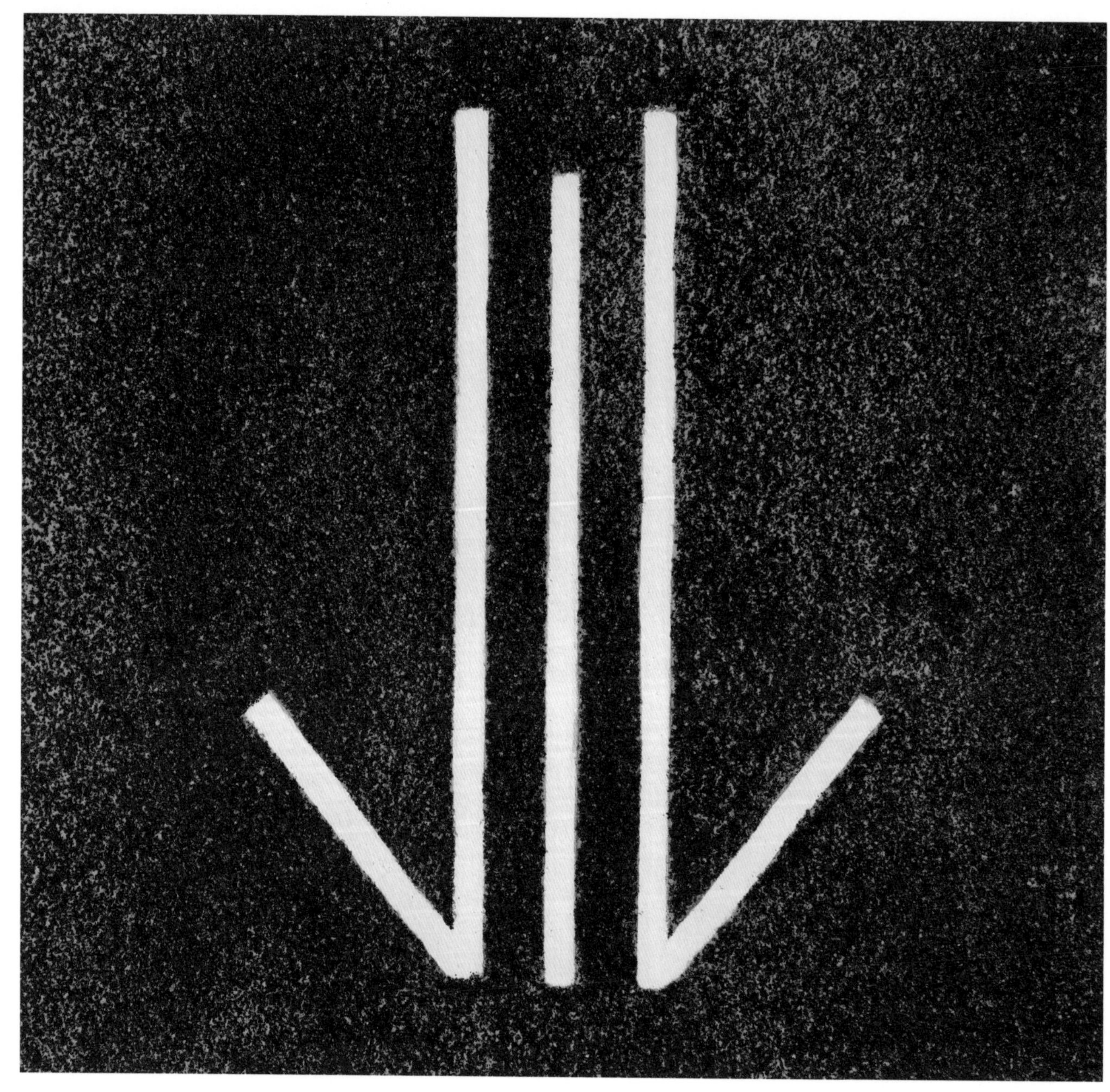

as a piece of driftwood in a river,
as a bat waiting for dusk,
or as a paper airplane through the air?

Would you rather

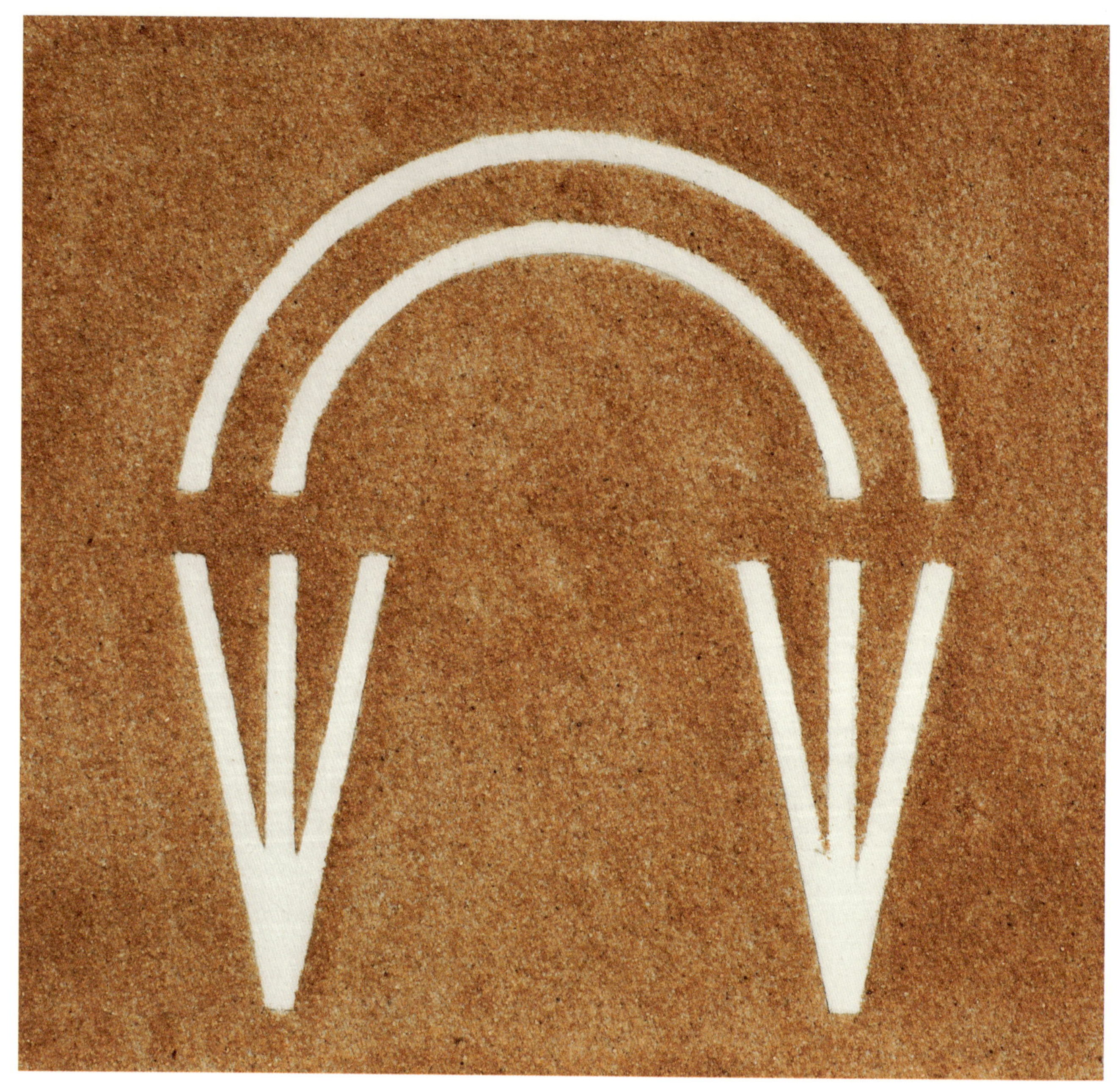

smell like a stored rubber tire,
a bunch of dried fragrant lavender blossoms,
freshly laundered sheets,
or a wet poodle?

Would you rather

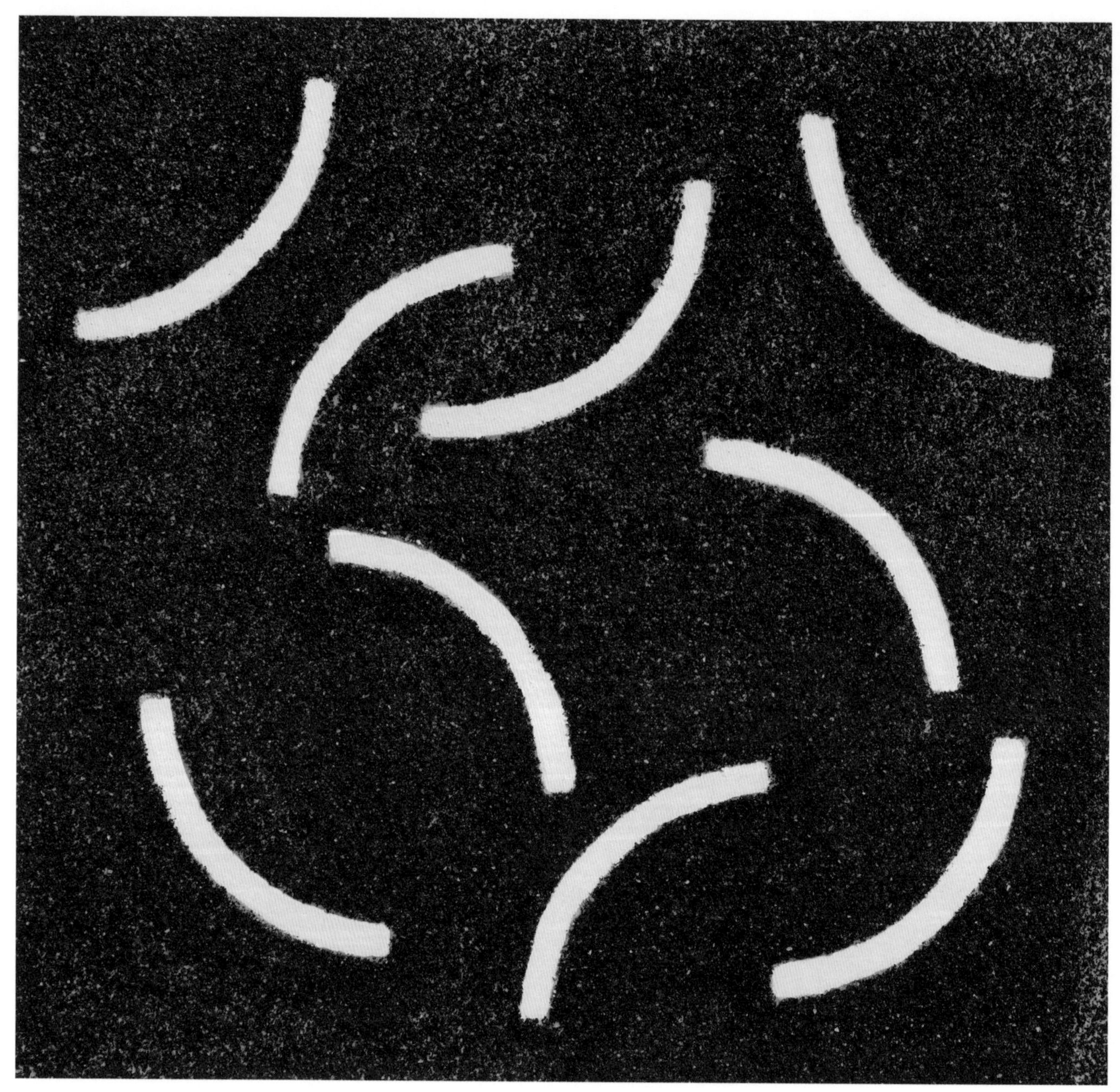

be a strand of bright pink candy floss,
a hide of pearly white rabbit fur,
or a pillow with buffalo check plaid?

Would you rather

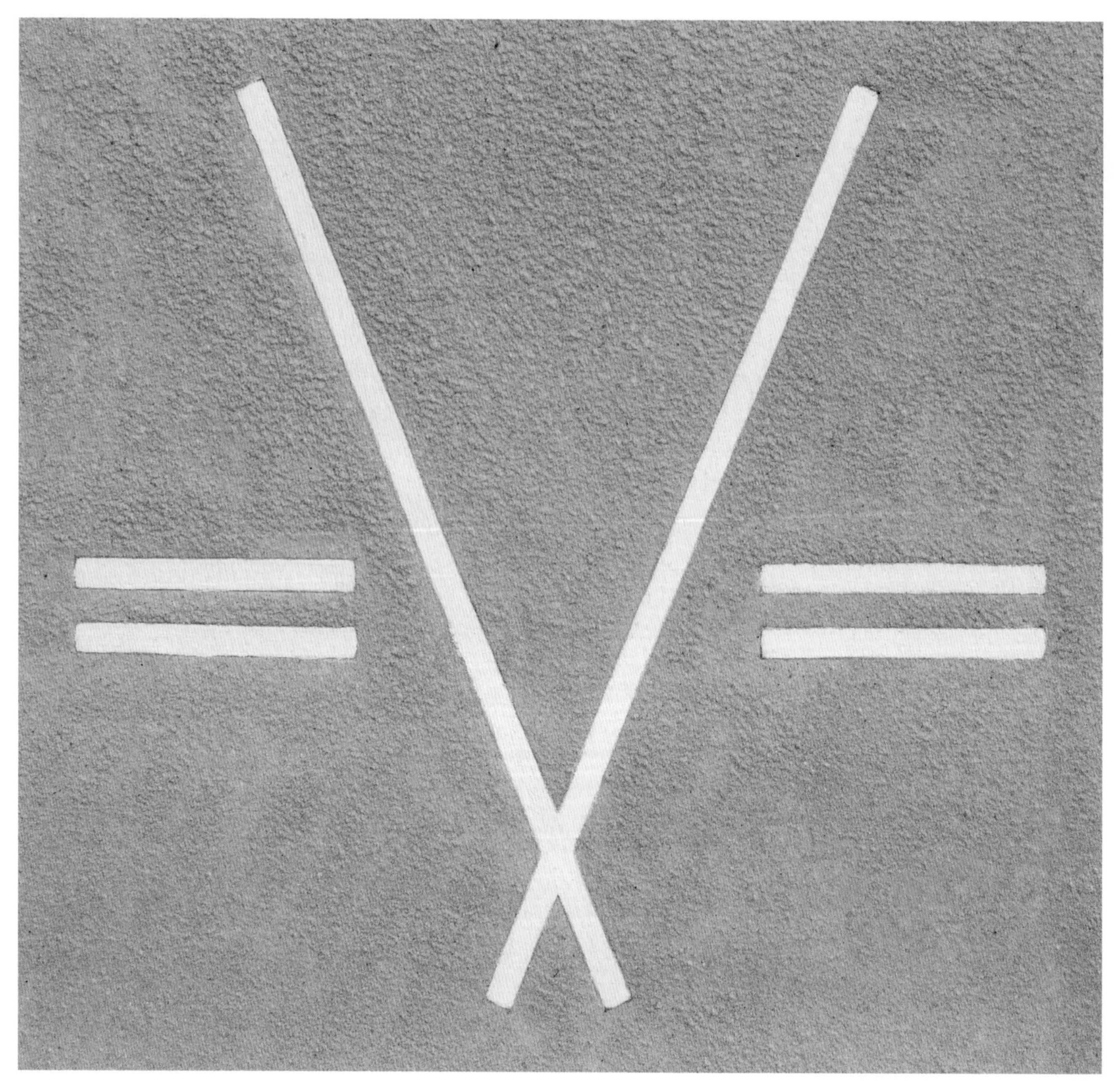

dam up a stream as a stone wall,
carry fleas as a cat,

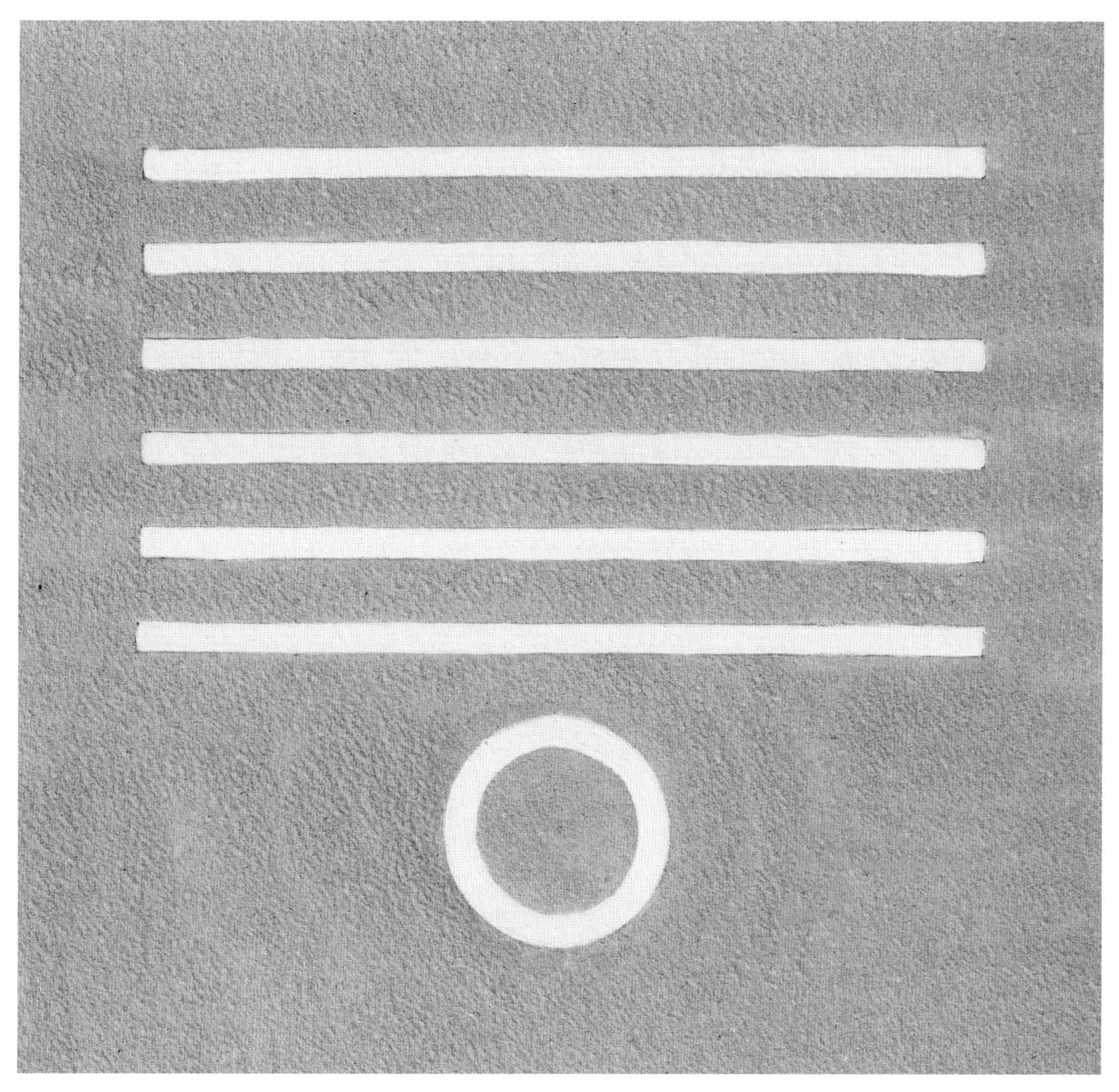

heat a house as a fire,
or hold up the sky as Atlas does?

Would you rather

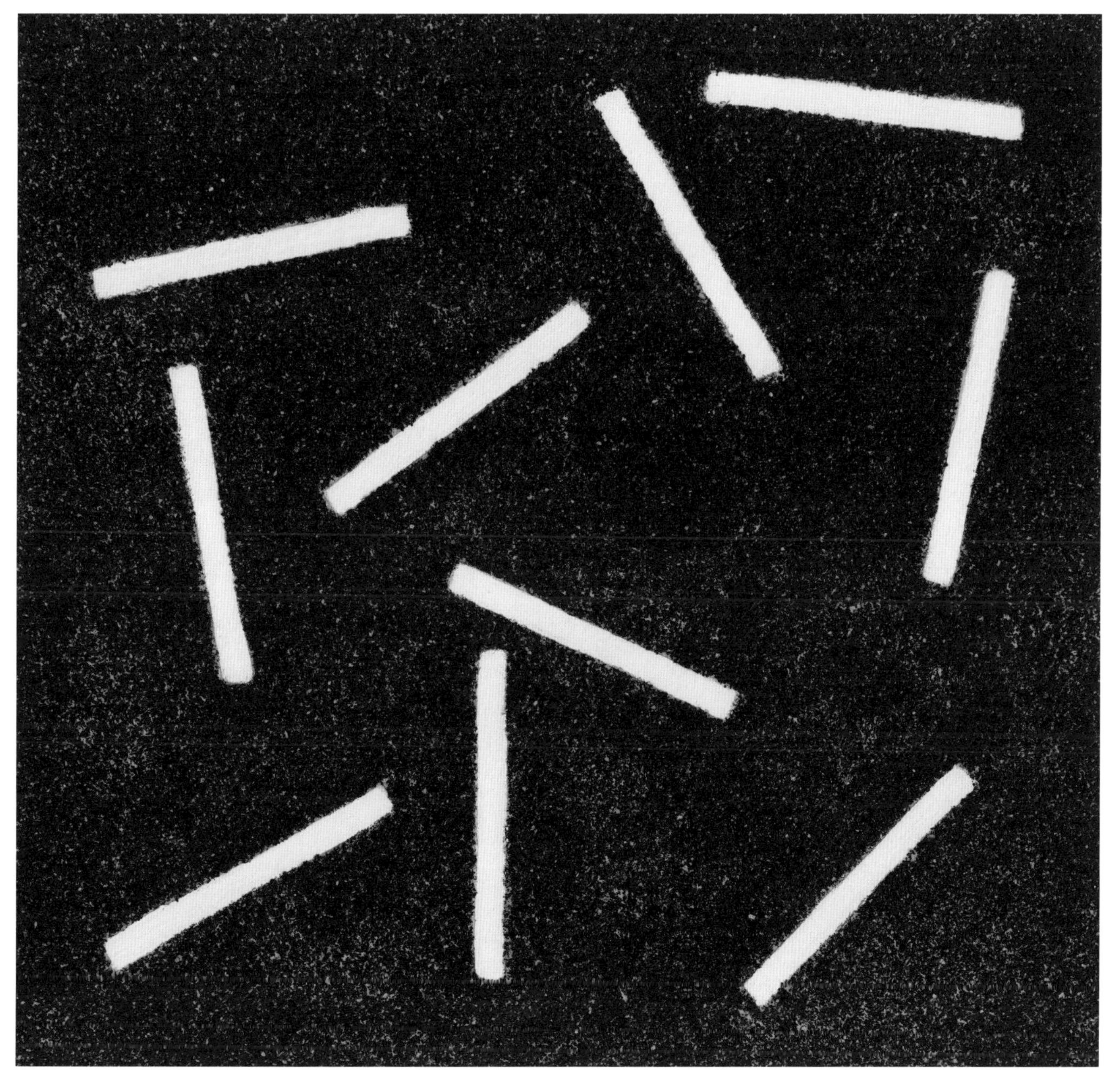

stick to the floor as a speck of blue paint,
stand in a glass as a dried-up paintbrush,
or lie in a wastepaper basket as a piece of crumpled-up paper?

Would you rather

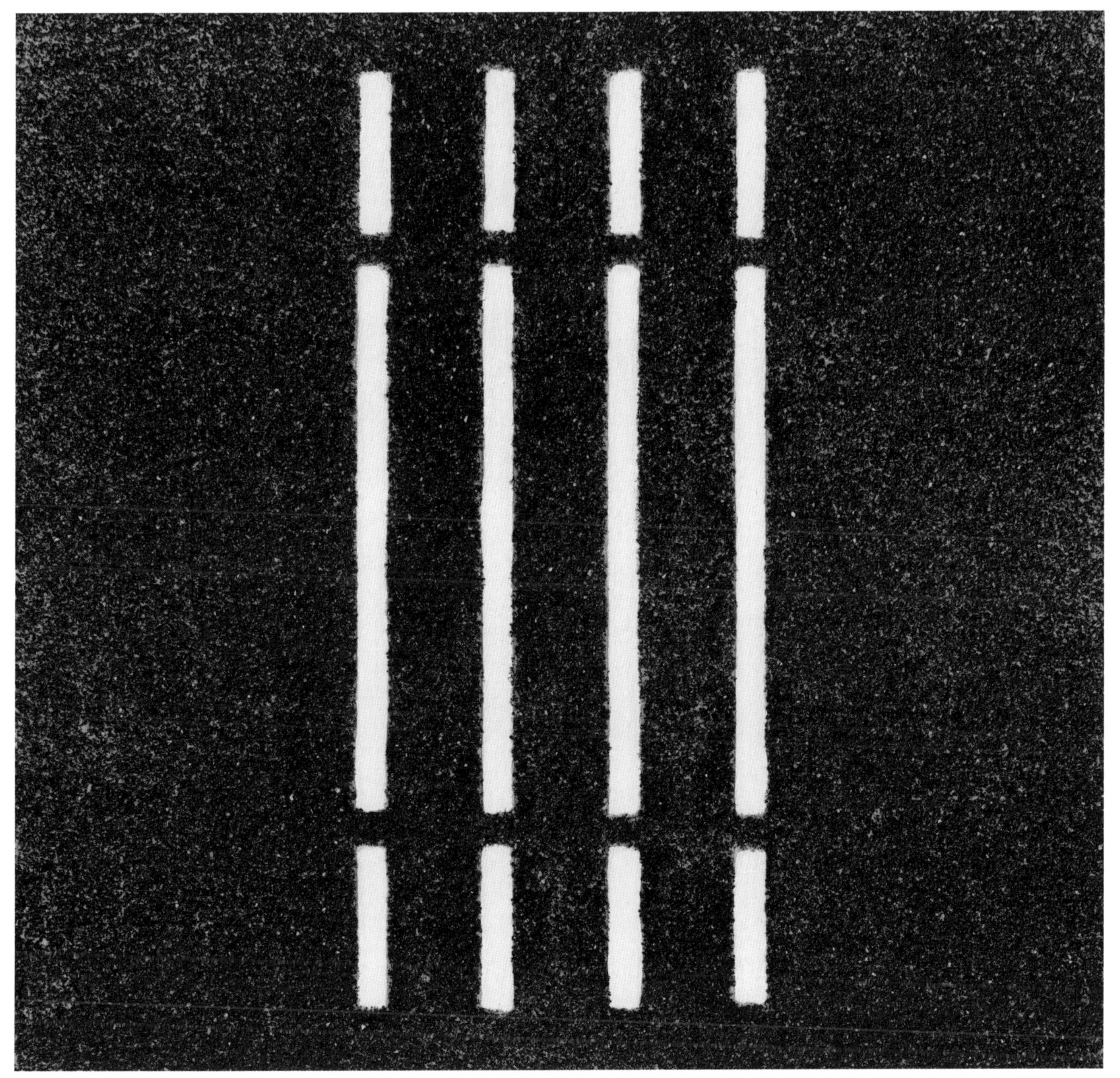

be a cat’s paw print on a birdhouse,
roller skates’ tracks on a parquet floor,
a busy motorway’s service lane,

or a jet stream's trail high up in the sky?

What would be worse for you

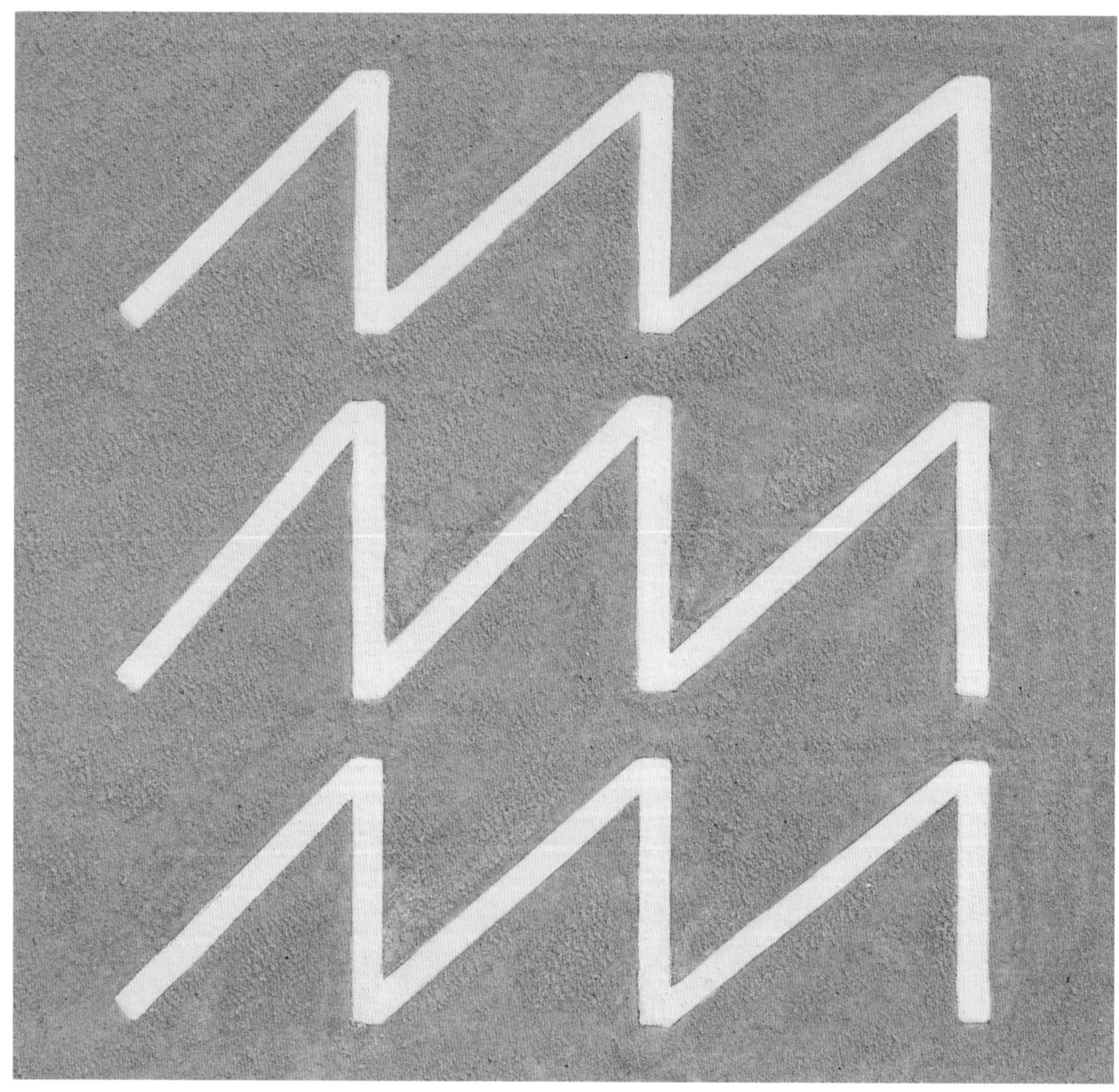

to be a sheep on its way to the butcher
or slaughterhouse waste on its way to the tinning factory?

Would you rather

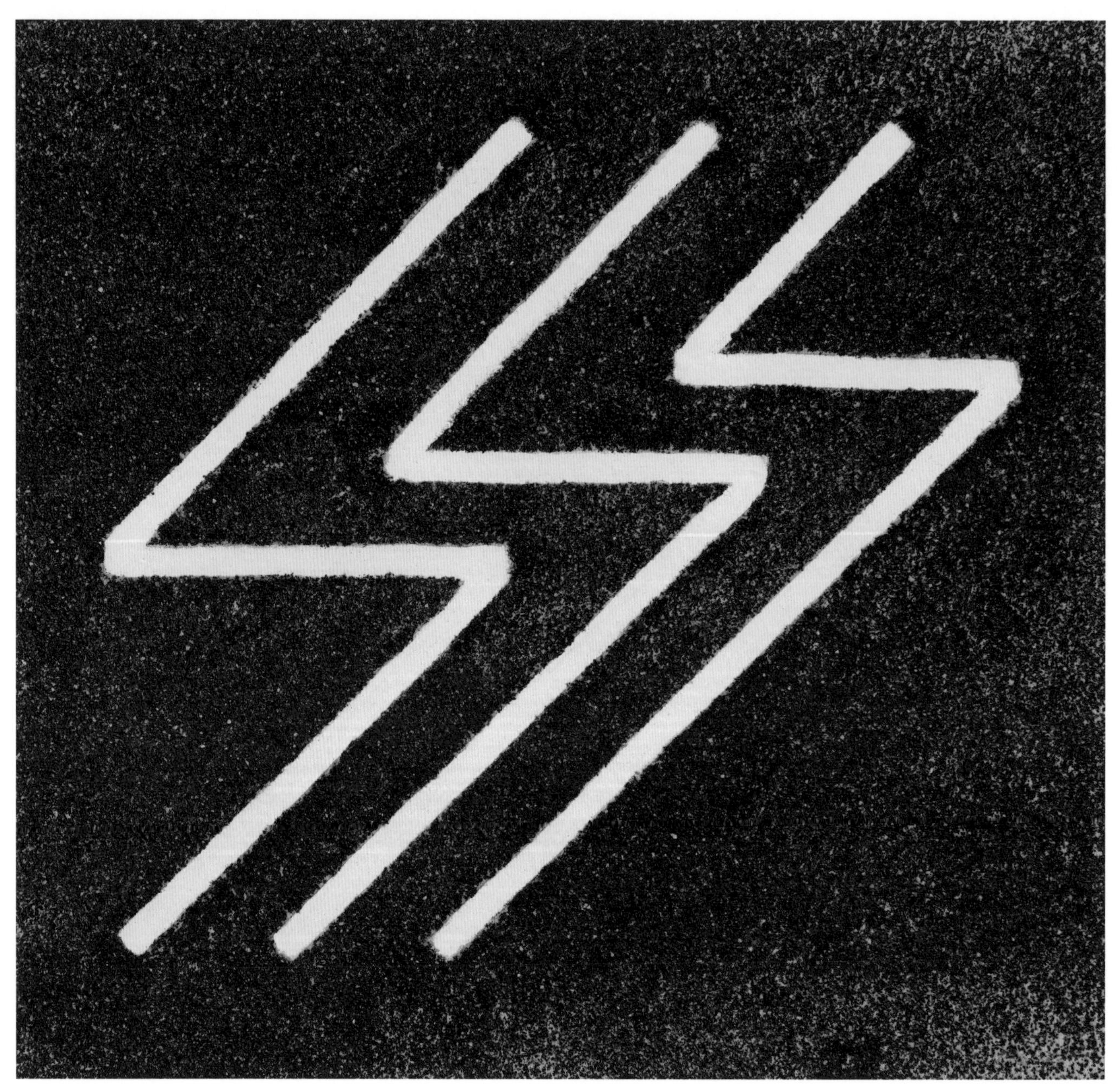

crash as a thunderstorm above a city,
roar as cheering from a football stadium,
or chirp as a cricket in summer?

Would you rather

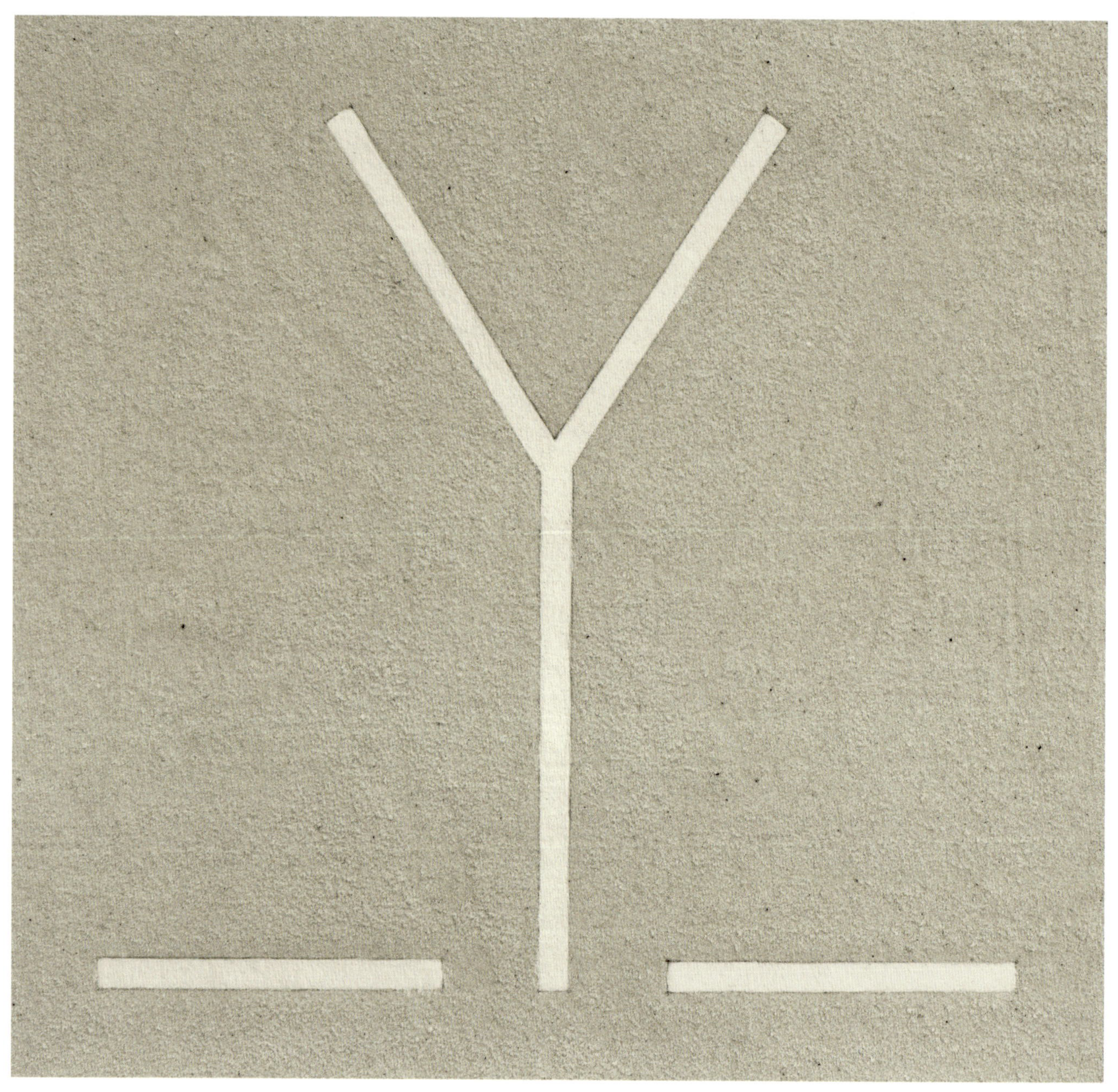

whirl through a pile of leaves as a breeze,

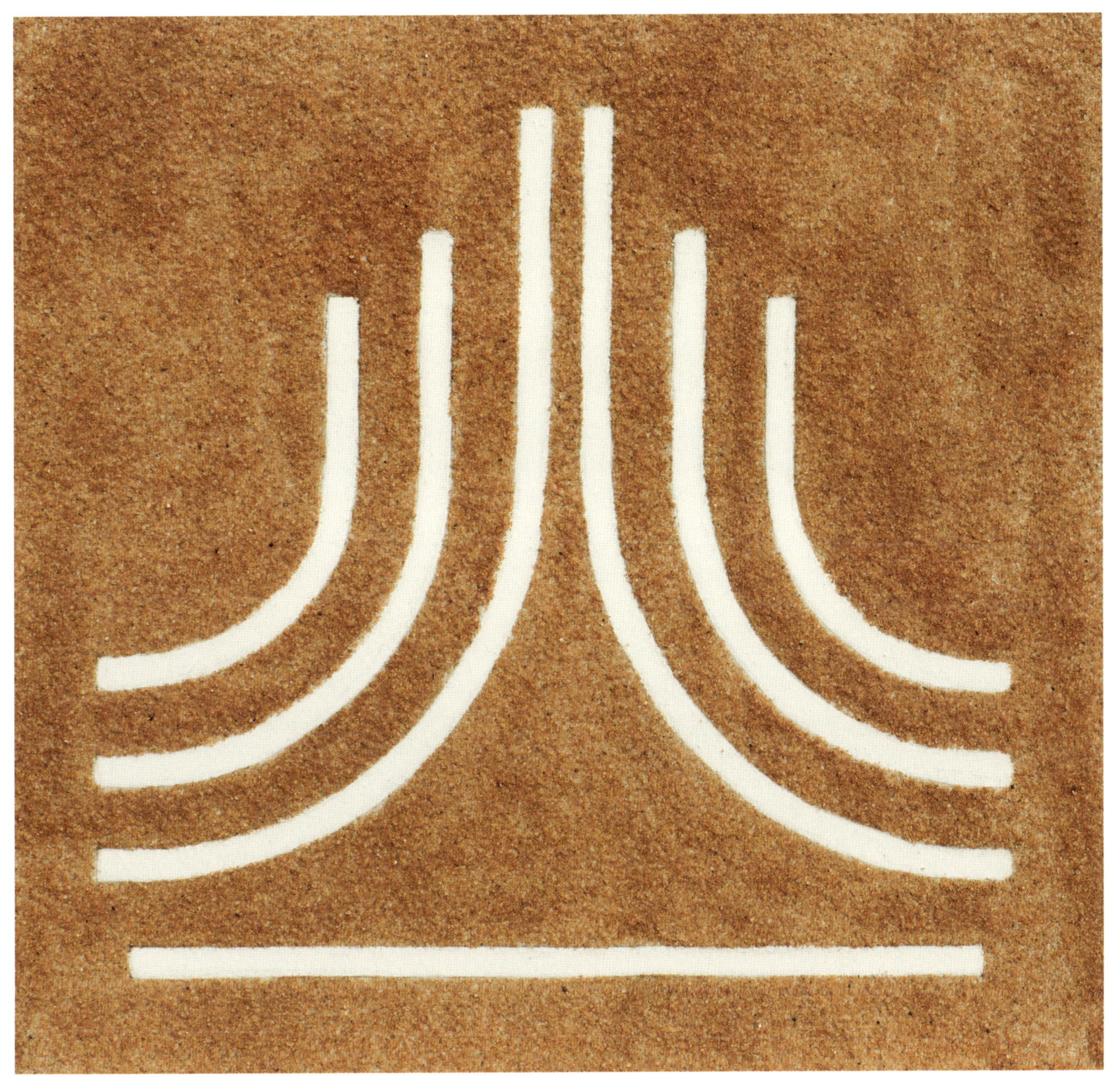

tickle a nose as a ray of sunlight,
dishevel hair as a gust of wind,
scratch a throat as a coughing fit,
nibble at a fir tree as a bark beetle,

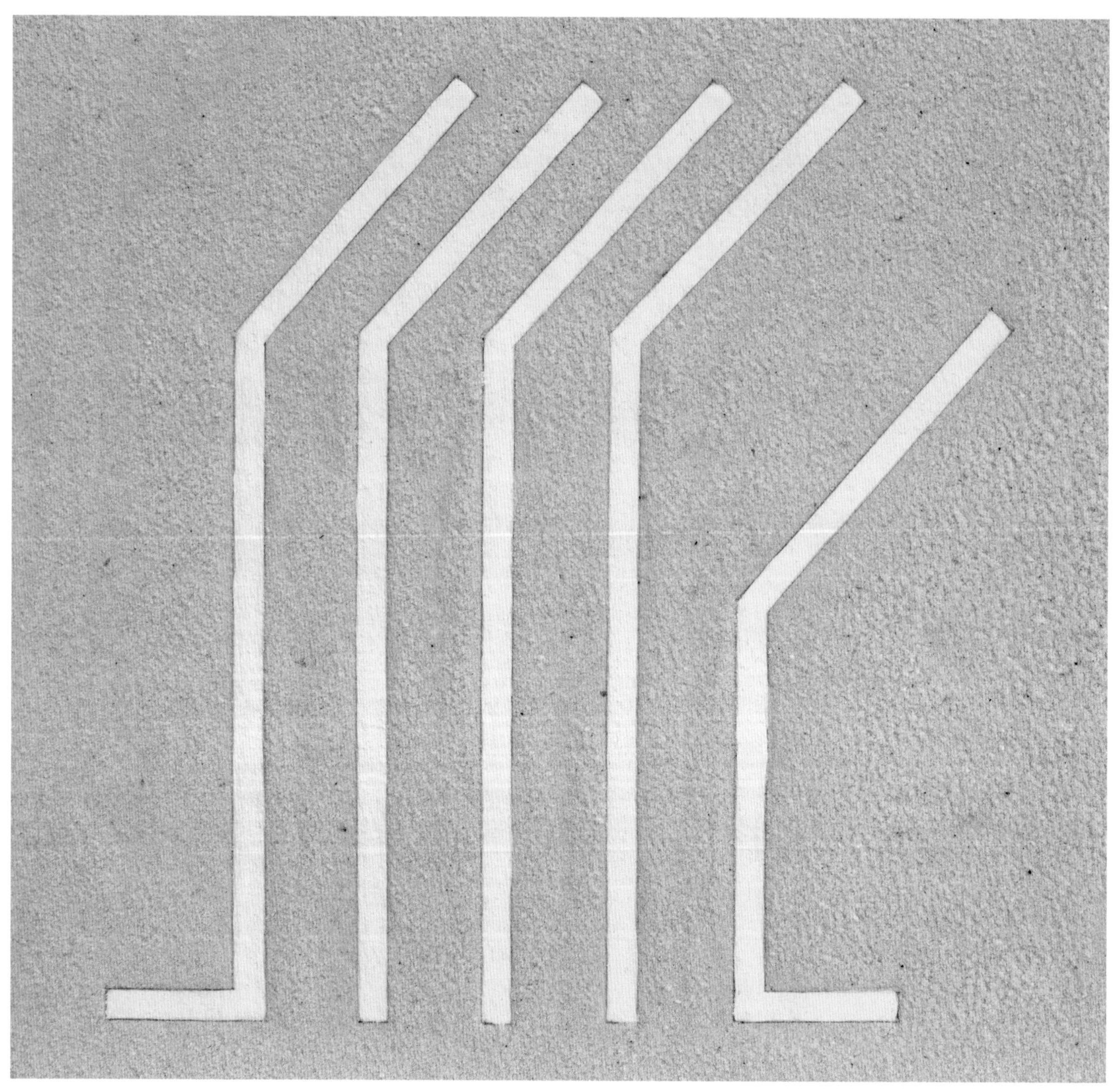

or turn a whole neighbourhood upside down as a hurricane?

Would you rather

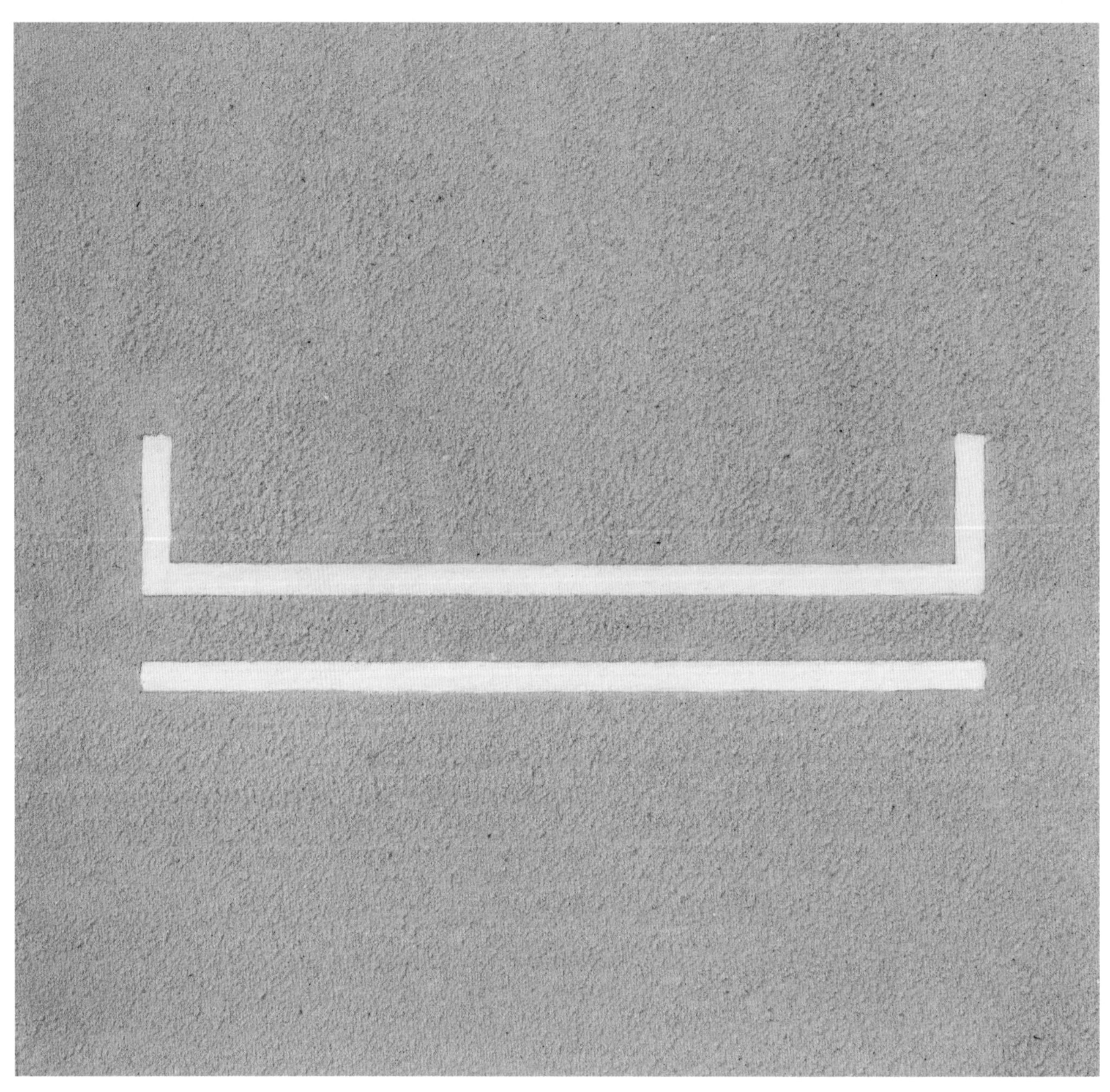

be a dingy sleeping mat of a homeless person,
a musty pot scrubber in the sink,

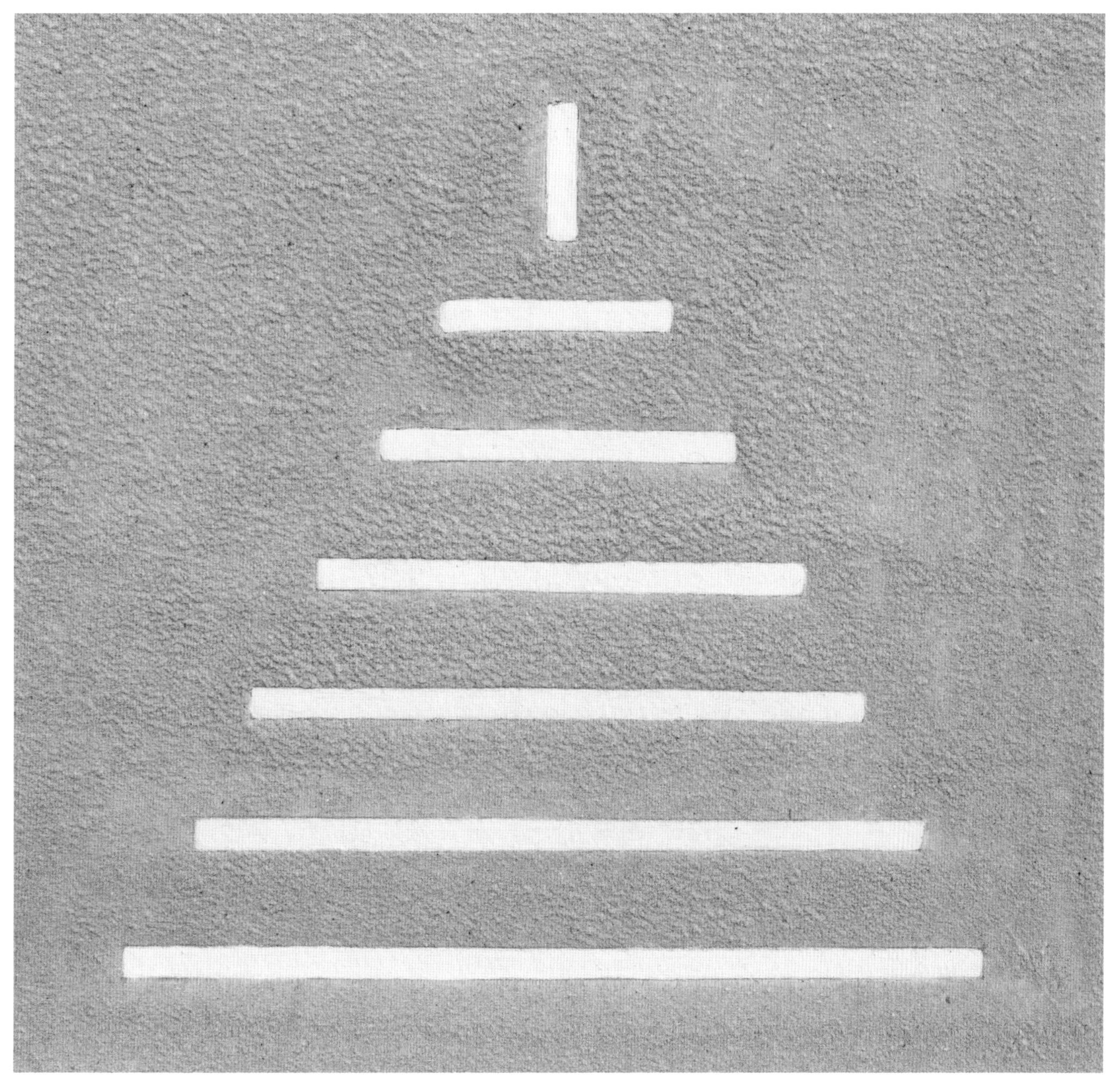

a rotting apple on top of a compost heap,
or a martin's droppings on a windshield?

Or would you rather be a hanky wadded up in
a caretaker's pocket?

Would you rather

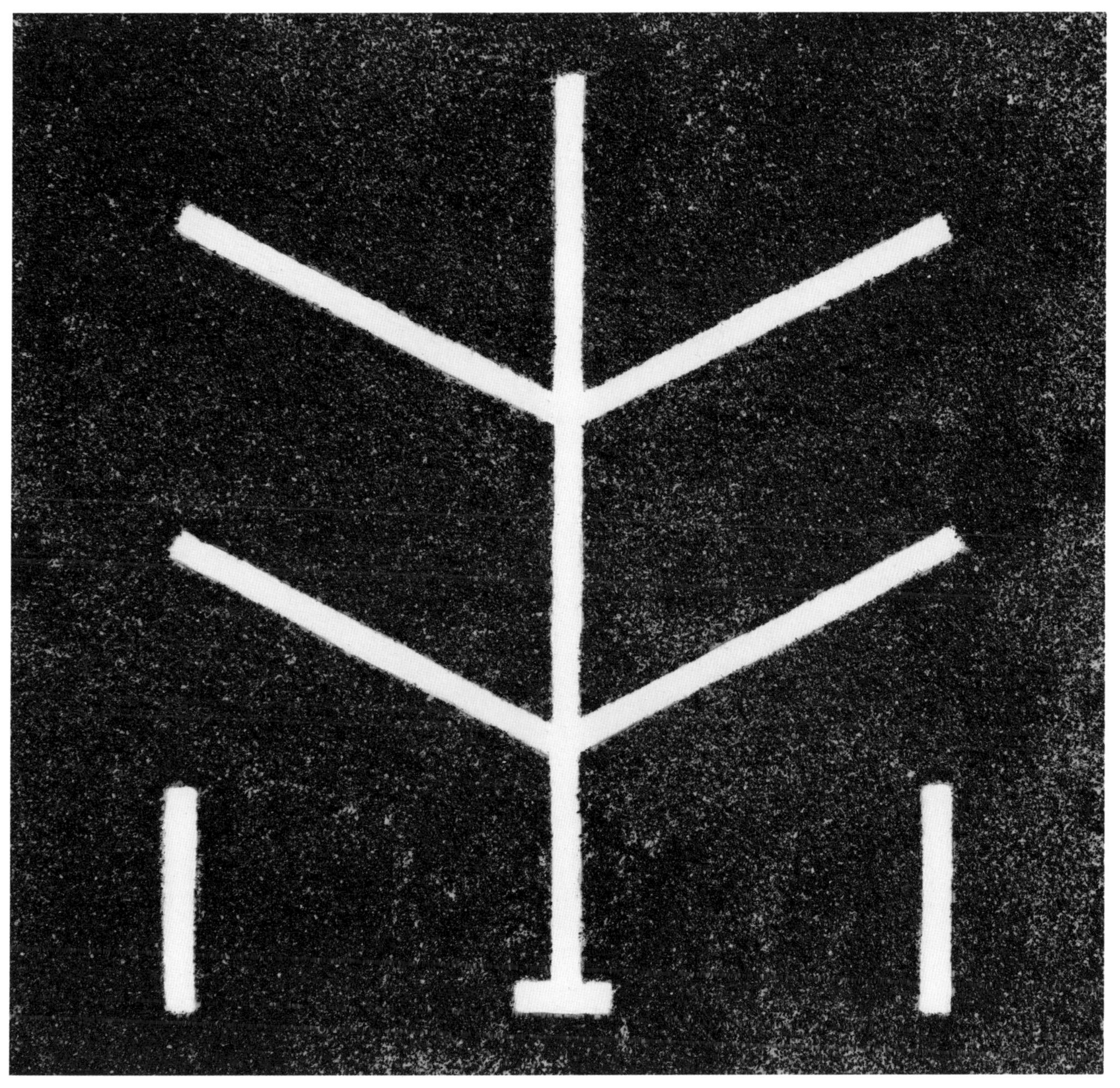

be a mouse with mountains of food stored away for the winter,
a goblin with gobs of presents to give away to children,
a barn with barrels of hay to feed the cows,

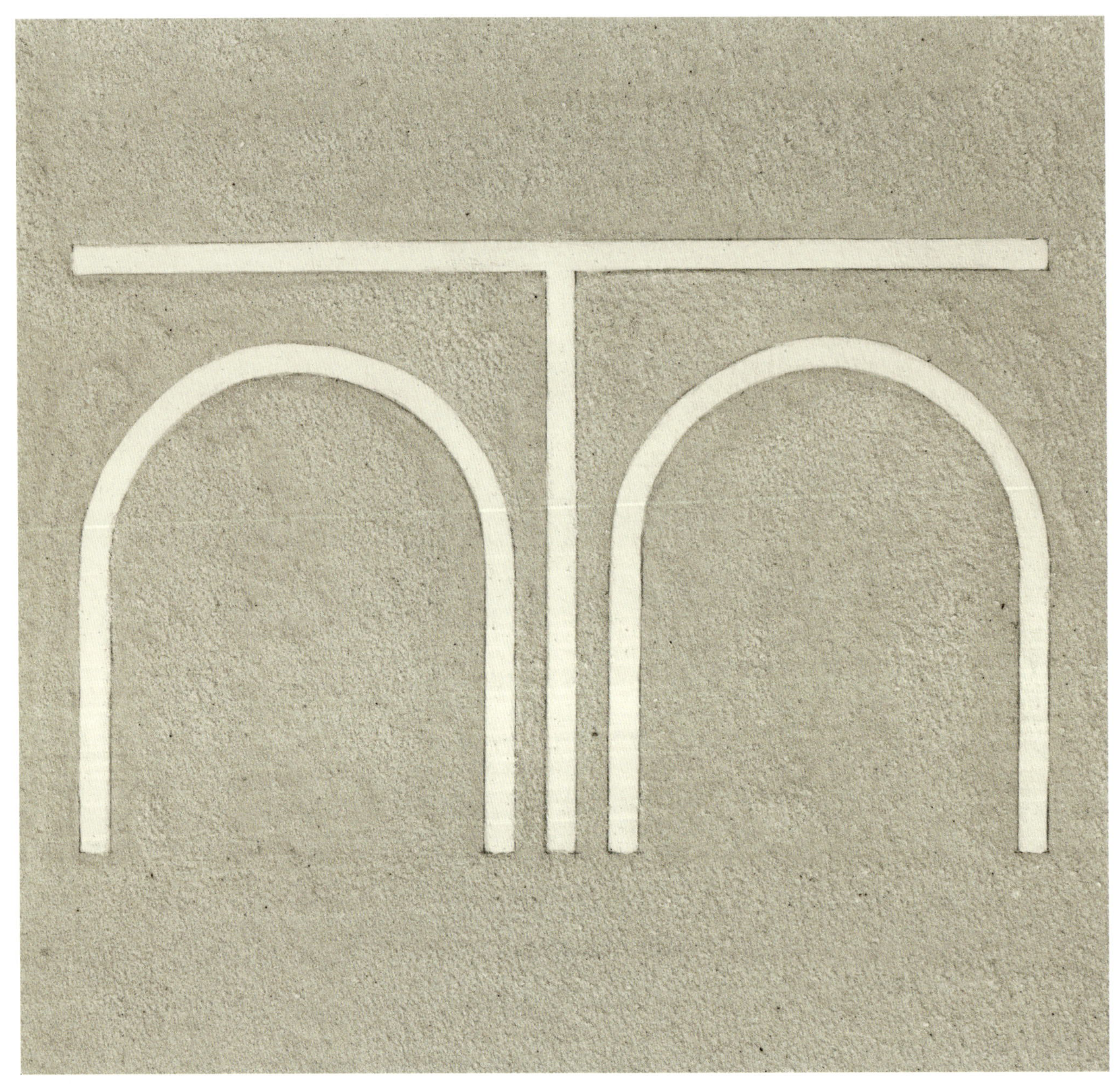

a truck with tons of goods from a supermarket,

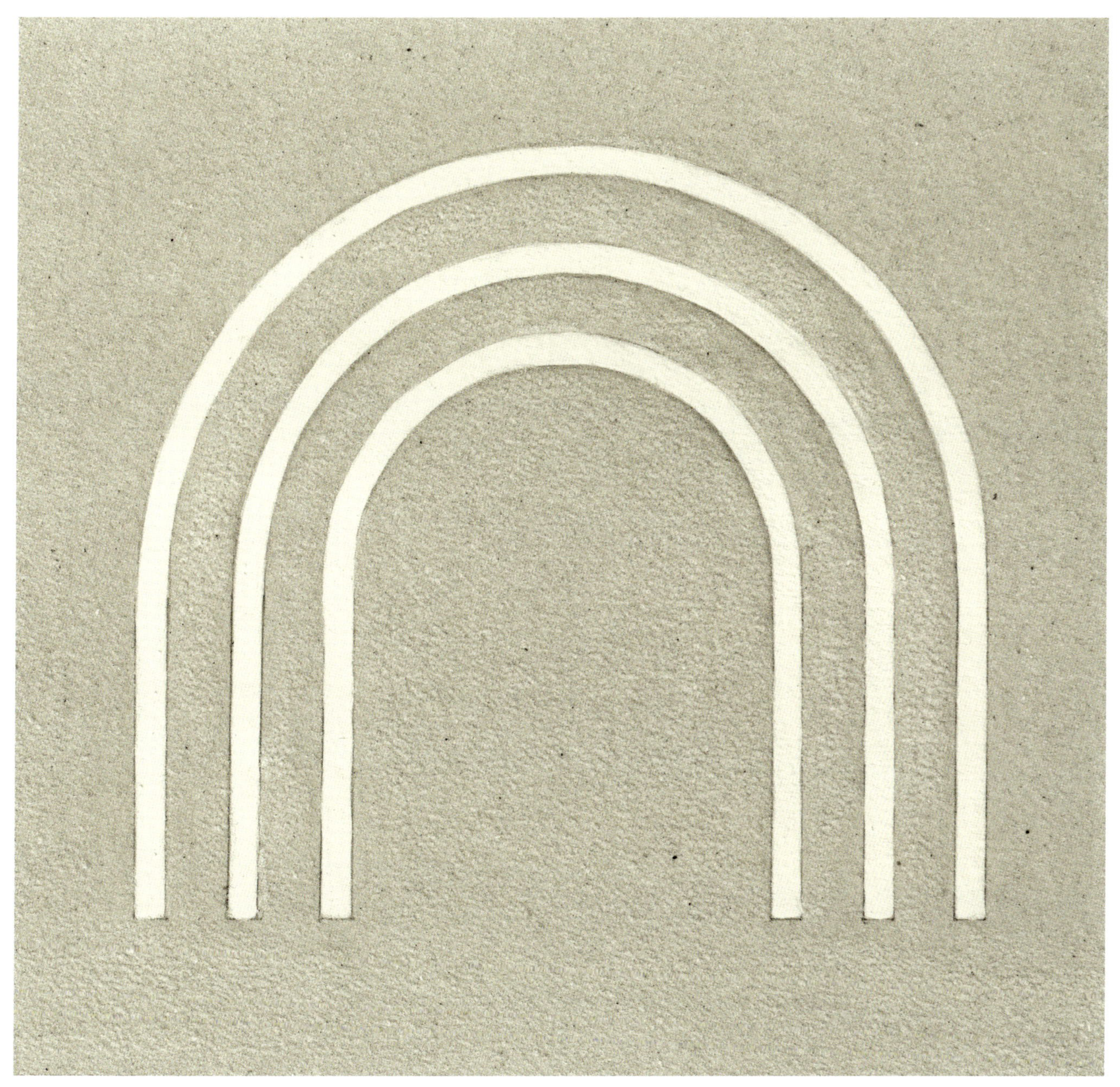

or a treasure hidden at the end of a rainbow?

Would you rather

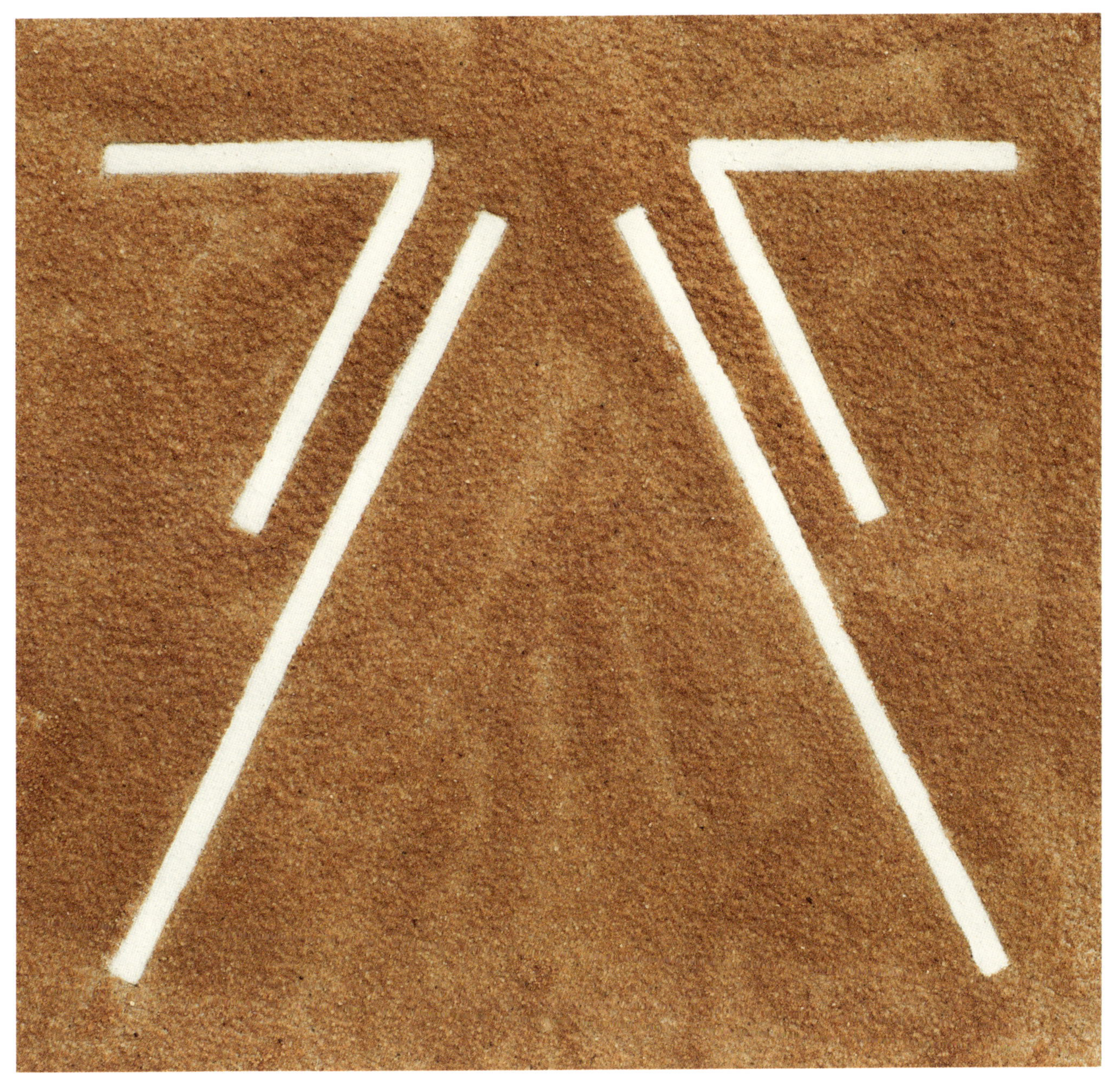

be a rare orchid in the rainforest,
the last dinosaur living in the Alps,
a racing bicycle as fast as lightning in a cellar,
a famous painting in a museum,

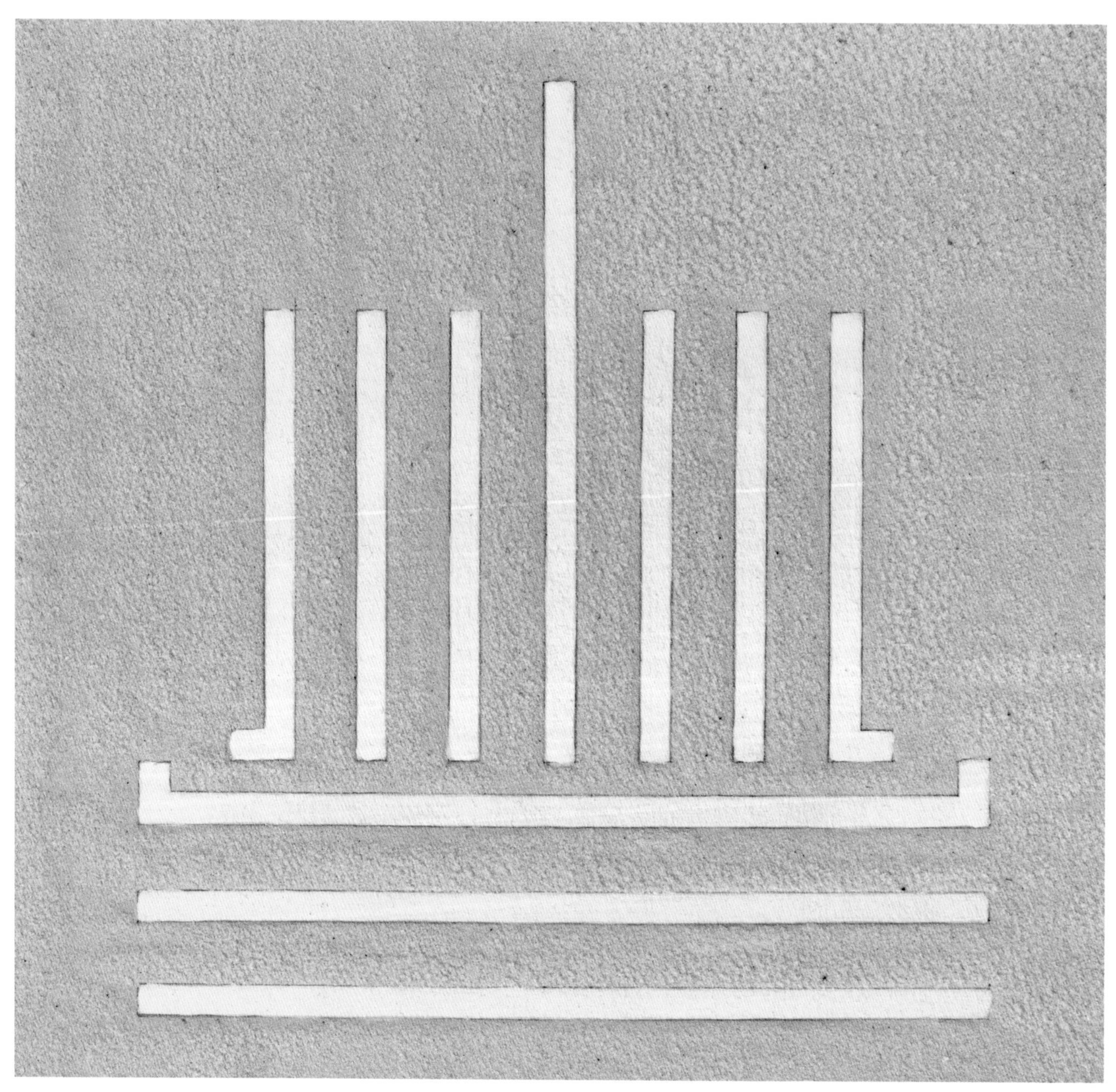

or a cake at a birthday party?

Would you rather

be a message in a bottle lying on the beach,

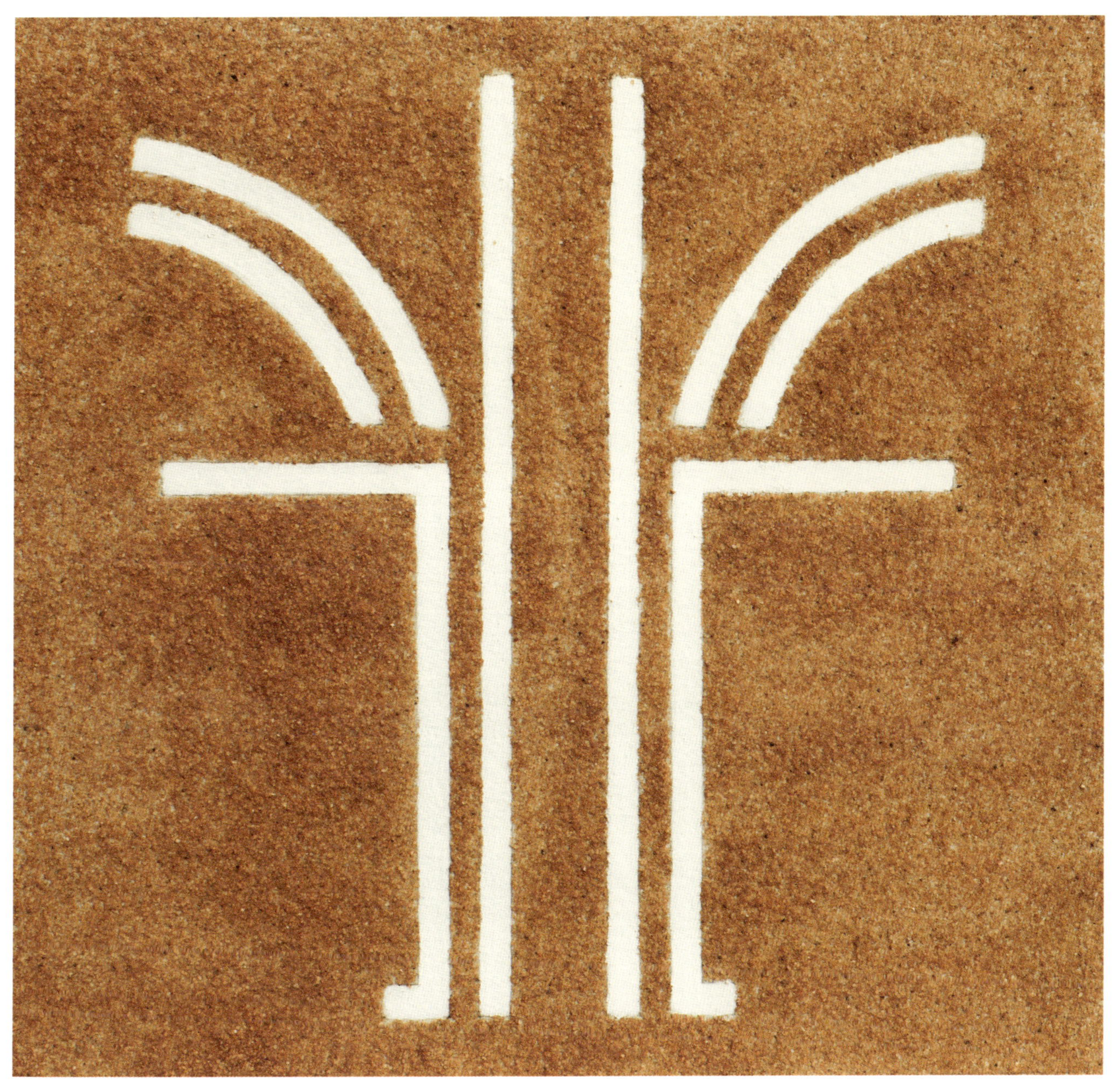

graffiti on the wall of a building,
horseshoe tracks on a meadow path,
a pop star's microphone,
or an announcement at a railway station?

Or would you rather be this book,
that you can fall asleep with while reading?

For Celestino, Kimi, Leolyn, Luis,
Lux, Mare, Merle, Nimo, Tula...

Text: Christoph Elias Meier & Mara Züst
Drawings: Carolina Cerbaro

Sand from Arizona (red), Isola d'Elba (black),
and the Ticino (white/beige)

Book Design: Carolina Cerbaro
Translation: Lux Züst
Text Editing: Linda Cassens Stoian
Image Editing: Tom Huber, Florian Zech (Kösel Media)
Printing and Binding: Kösel GmbH & Co.

Kindly supported by
Erna und Curt Burgauer Stiftung
Stadt Zürich Kultur

First Edition 500 copies

Published by Nieves

ISBN 978-3-905999-84-6
Printed in Germany

www.nievesbooks.com